Special Symbols:

This book is organized to guide the individual through the training. In addition to the Notes section there are a number of symbols used to help the participant throughout the presentation and workshop. For your convenience these symbols are repeated at the introduction of each section of this workbook.

Suggestion:

This symbol represents a suggestion or is a general statement relating to facilitation of the training.

Tip:

This symbol represents a tip to the Facilitator and is specific to the concept that the Facilitator is presenting.

Question:

This symbol represents a question that may be asked to the Facilitator or to the participants in the workshop. It is intended to foster interaction during the training.

T0138998

Table of Contents

Section 1

5S & Lean Operations 1

Section 2

5S & Organization: Each Piece of the Puzzle 19

Section 3

5S & Teamwork 39

5S & Lean Operations

Participant Workbook

In this Section

- Learn the context of 5S
- Discover how 5S fits into improvement projects
- Study the 7 Wastes of Operations

Participant Workbook Provided To:

_____

Suggestion

Tip

Question

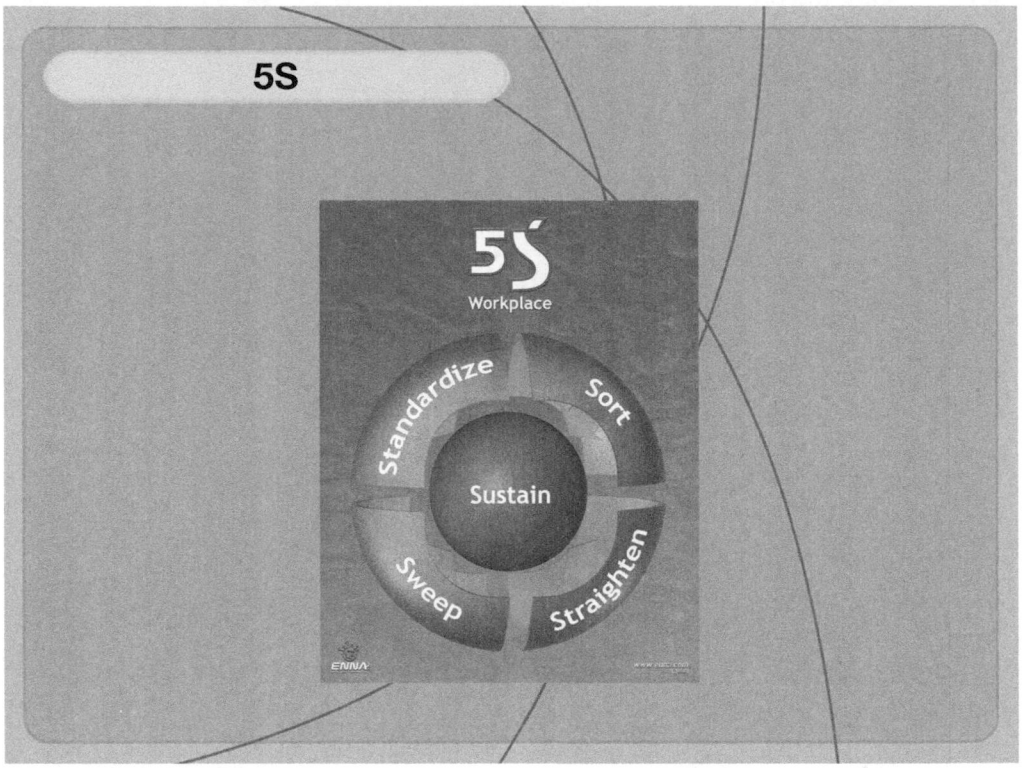

Notes, Slide 1:

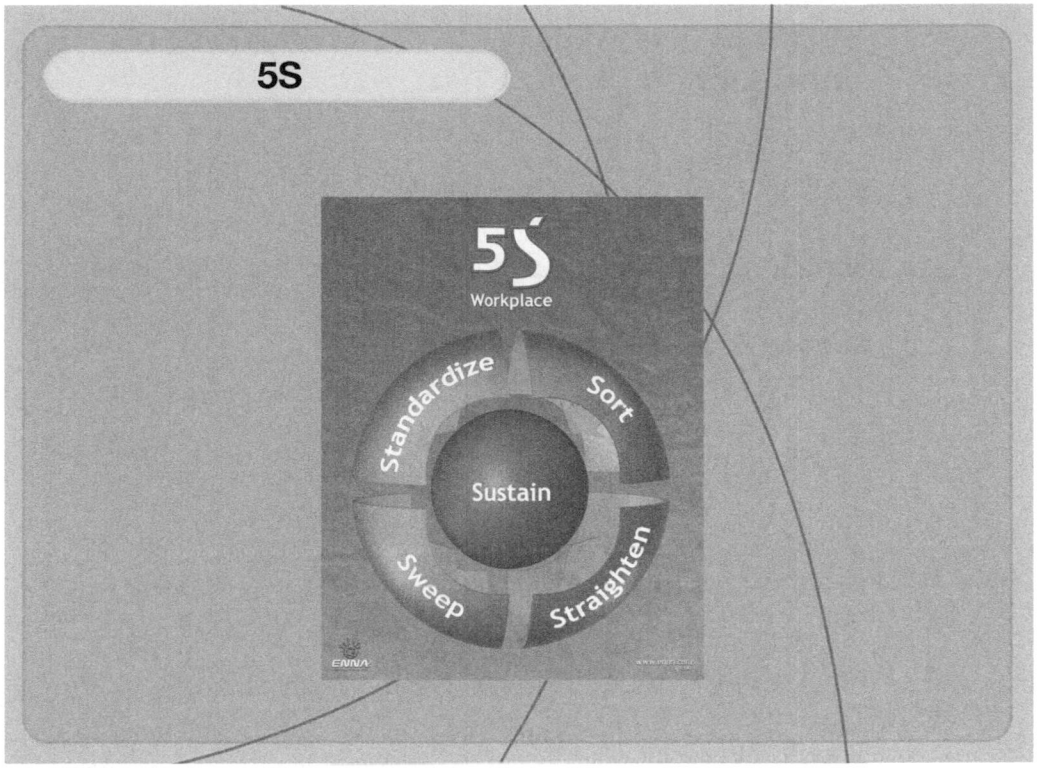

Notes, Slide 1 continued:

Tip:
Pay particular attention to the Facilitator when learning about a clean operation.

Question:

What do people generally think of an operation that is clean?

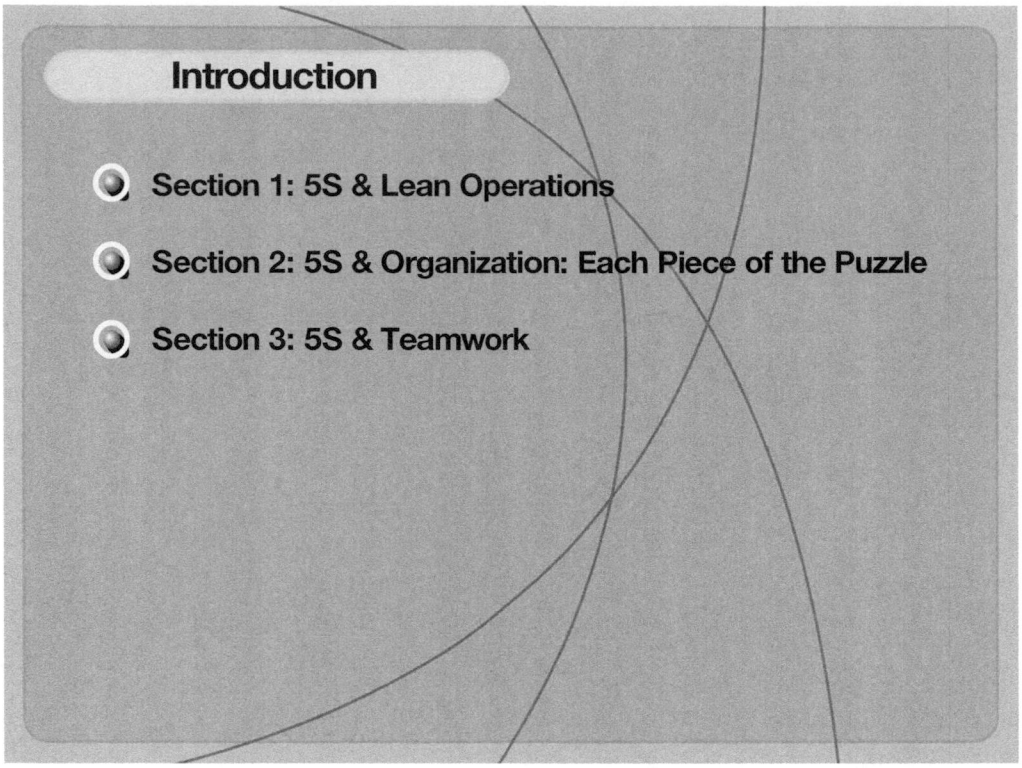

Notes, Slide 2:

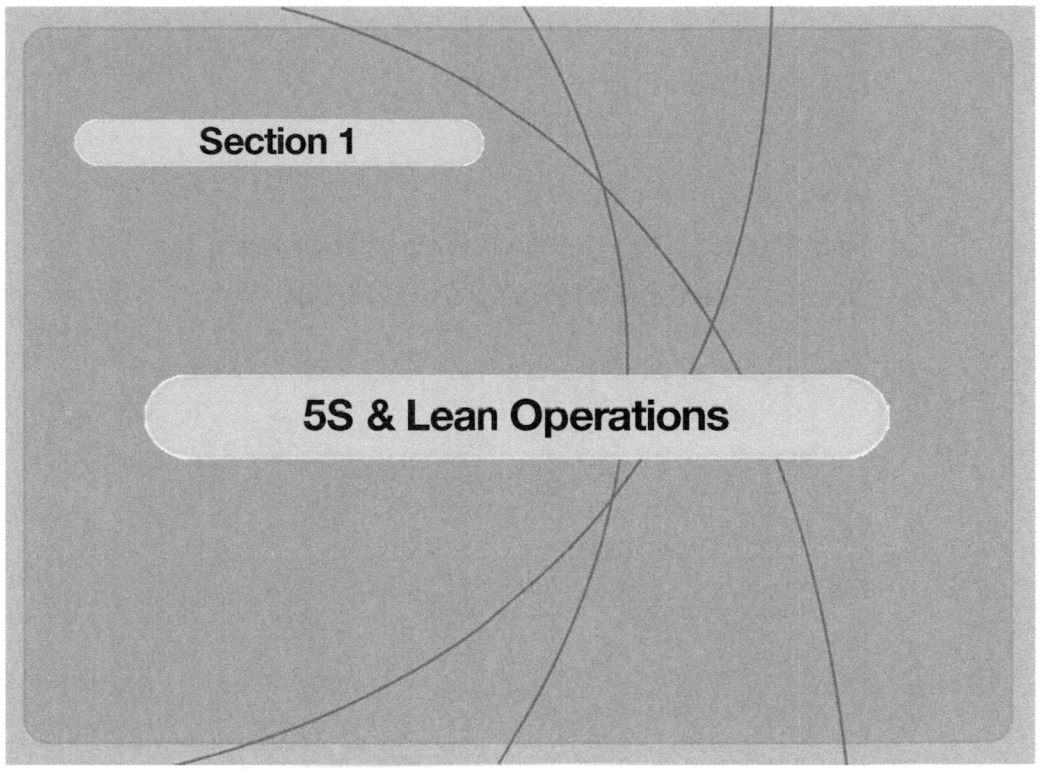

Notes, Slide 3:

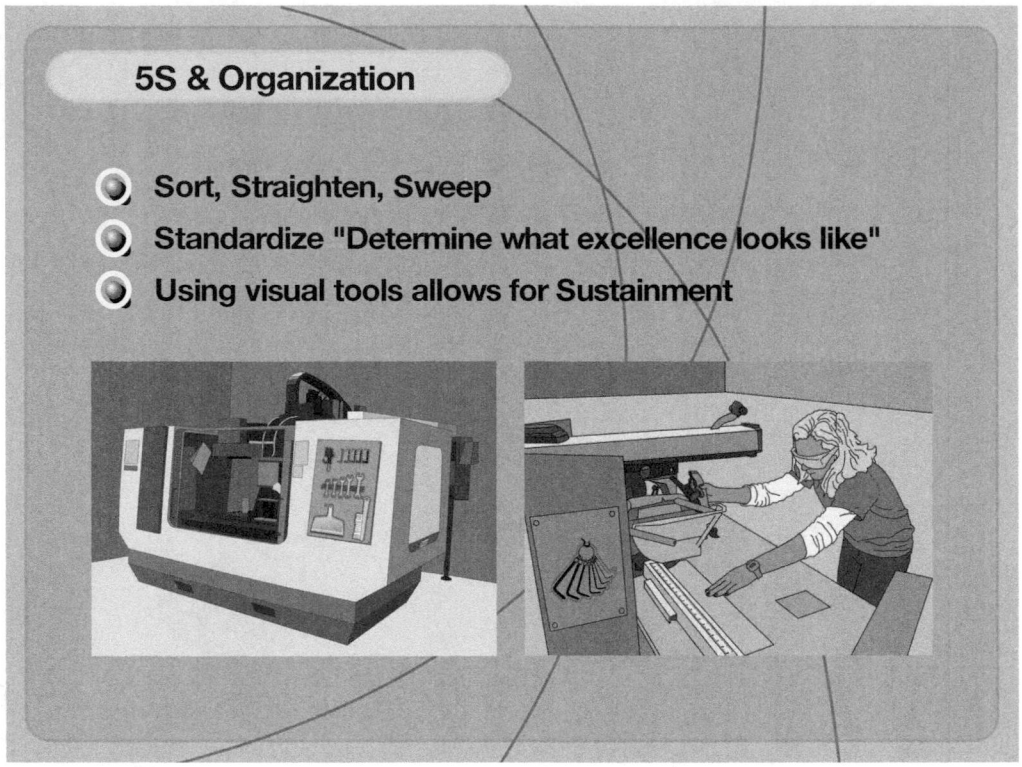

Notes, Slide 4:

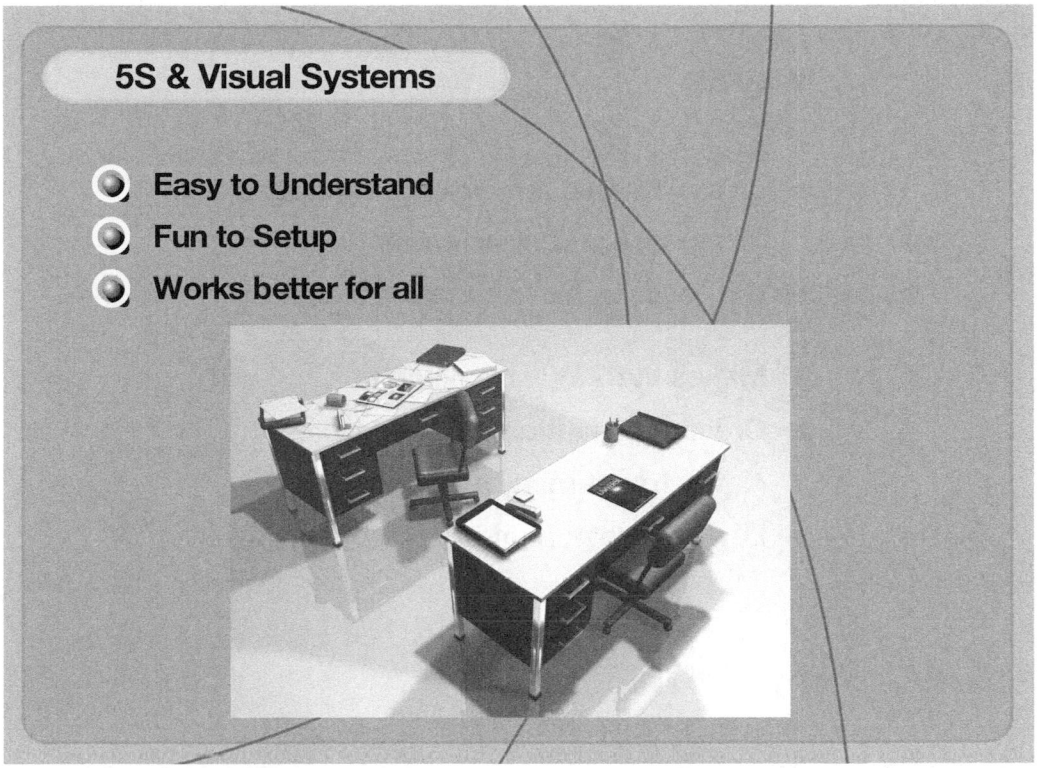

Notes, Slide 5:

Question:

Can you think of any kind of job that may require the need to be visual?

Why 5S

- Allows us to maintain a more organized area
- Able to clean less and clean easier
- Makes our work area more productive
  - Makes the 7 Wastes obvious
  - Creates a standard for improvement
  - A way to get many people involved
  - Low real cost, high-impact for company

Notes, Slide 6:

Question:

Why are we doing 5S?

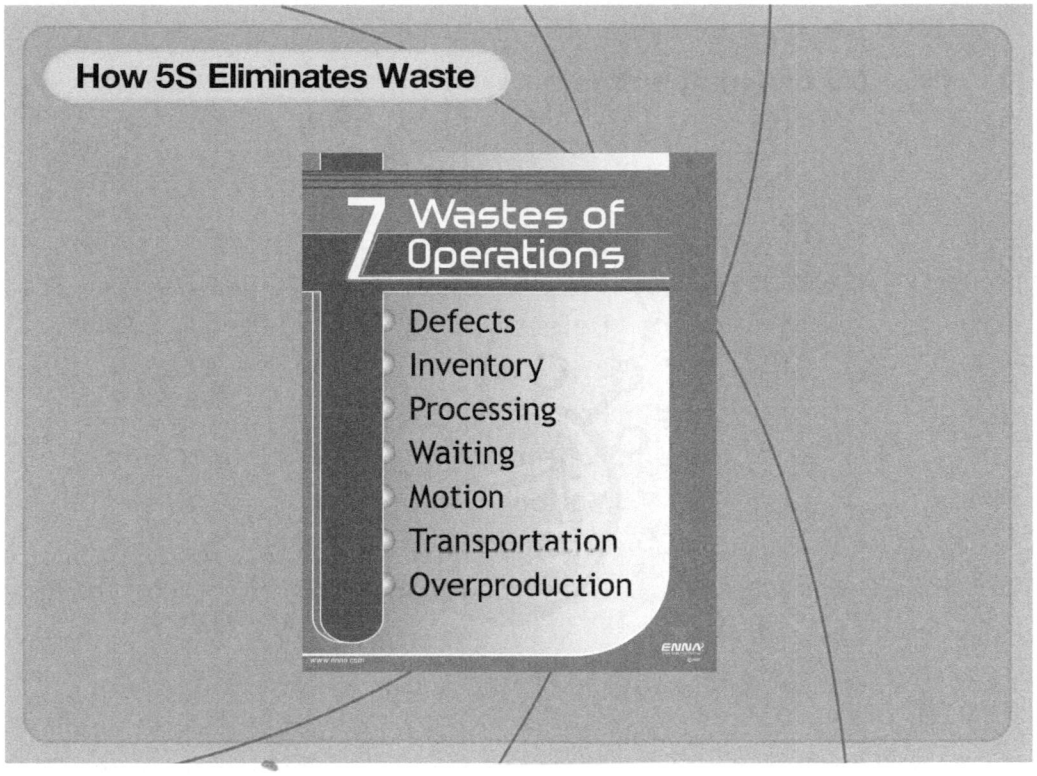

Notes, Slide 7:

Tip:
Focus on the 7 Wastes and what the definitions are.

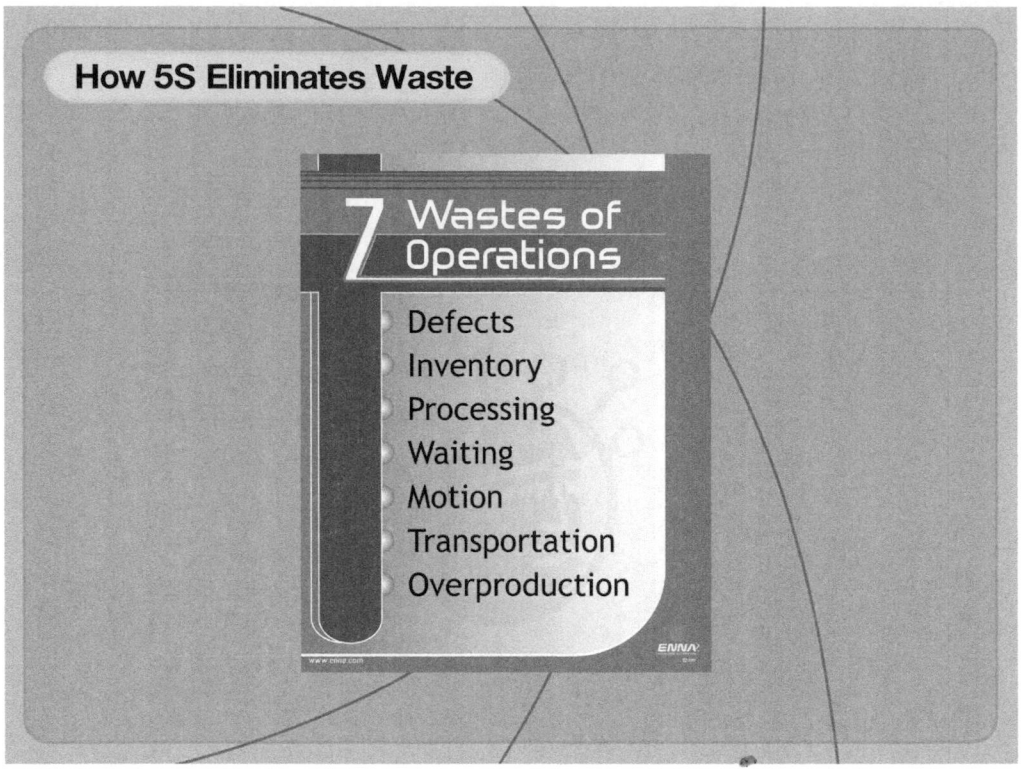

Notes, Slide 7 continued:

Tip:
The 7 Wastes are a fundamental building block of 5S. Ask the facilitator to fully explain the wastes so that you understand them completely.

Defects

Making bad parts, having scrap, wrong information, and/or having to rework items.

Possible Causes:

- **Batch Processing**
- **Quality materials**
- **Questionable product design**
- **Poor work instructions**

Notes, Slide 8:

_____

_____

_____

_____

Waste Definition: _____

_____

Additional Example: _____

_____

Inventory

Any material in the area other than what is immediately needed for the next process, stage, or step.

Possible Causes:

- Long lead times
- Supplier reliability
- Reward based on output
- Just-in-case logic
- Poor scheduling
- Unknown market demand

Notes, Slide 9:

_____

_____

_____

_____

Waste Definition: _____

_____

Additional Example: _____

_____

Question:

What are the three stages that inventory lives as in your company?

_____

_____

_____

Processing

Activity that adds no value to the product or service from the viewpoint of the internal/external customer.

Possible Causes:

- **Too much paperwork**
- **No communication**
- **Too many steps**
- **Next customer s needs not known**

Notes, Slide 10:

Tip:
This is the hardest waste to find. However, the solution is simple. If you think about it, if it is truly a waste of over processing, then the ultimate solution is to find a way to not do it.

Waste Definition: _____

Additional Example: _____

Waiting

Is created when materials, information, machines, or approvals are not ready for the person.

Possible Causes:

- **Machine breakdown**
- **Work load variance**
- **Quality issues**
- **Too much work**

Notes, Slide 11:

_____

_____

_____

_____

Waste Definition: _____

_____

Additional Example: _____

_____

Tip:
Try purposely waiting rather than doing something. It is hard to wait.

Question:

What are some times that you have waited? What are you waiting for?

_____

_____

_____

Motion

Any movement that does not add value to the product or service.

Possible Causes:

- Lack of process design
- No standard work methods
- Design of work area
- Too much in an area

Notes, Slide 12:

_____

_____

_____

_____

Waste Definition: _____

_____

Additional Example: _____

_____

Transportation

Moving materials from one area to another area.

Possible Causes:

- Batch production systems
- WIP storage
- Layout of the facility
- Staging stock
- Utilization of forklifts

Notes, Slide 13:

_____

_____

_____

_____

Waste Definition: _____

_____

Additional Example: _____

_____

Overproduction

Making more components/products than the next process (or internal/external customer) requires.

Possible Causes:

- Just-in-case logic
- Focus on machine only
- Setup times
- Keep working
- Demand issues

Notes, Slide 14:

Tip:
Operations should look at ways to only produce what is truly needed. Anything more will result in loss of efficiency and effectiveness.

Waste Definition: _____

Additional Example: _____

Question:

Why is overproduction so detrimental to an organization?

5S & Lean Operations

Most, if not all, of the essential tools of Lean have the 5S as the key building blocks.

Examples:

- TPM
- Kanban
- SMED
- Visual Management
- Office Kaizen

Notes, Slide 15:

5S & Organization: Each Piece of the Puzzle

Participant Workbook

In this Section

- The meaning behind 5S
- Applying 5S in your area and environment
- The five elements of 5S
- Guide for participants through the proper sequence of learning 5S

Suggestion

Tip

Question

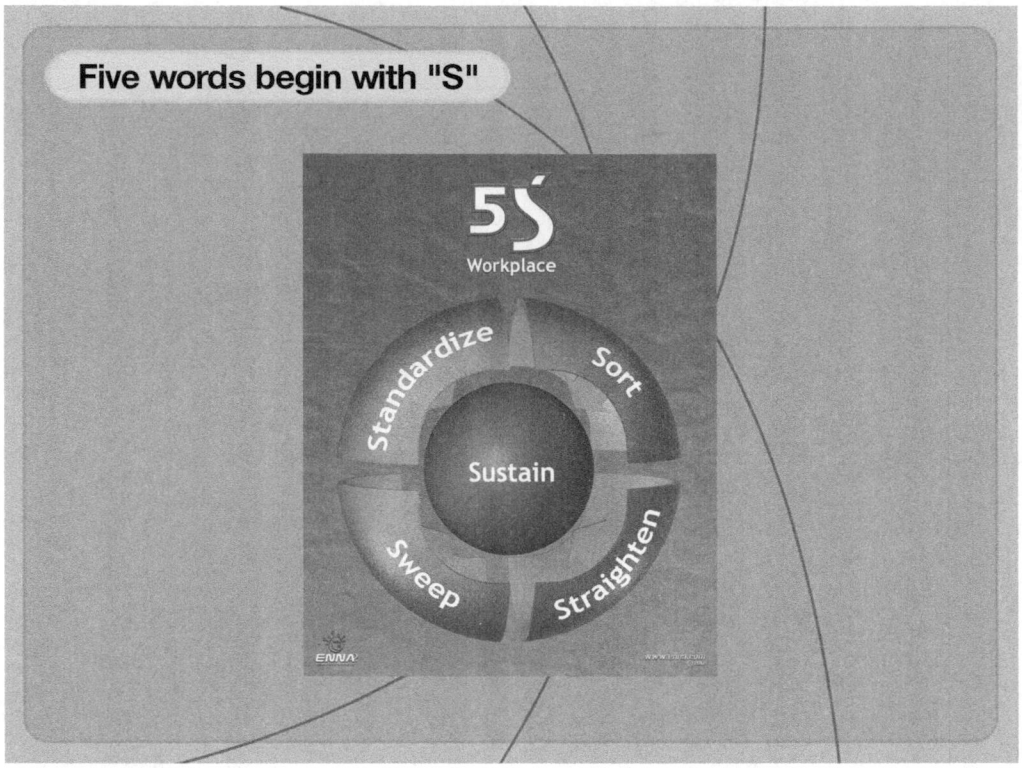

Notes, Slide 17:

Question:

How many S's were there originally and which company founded the term?

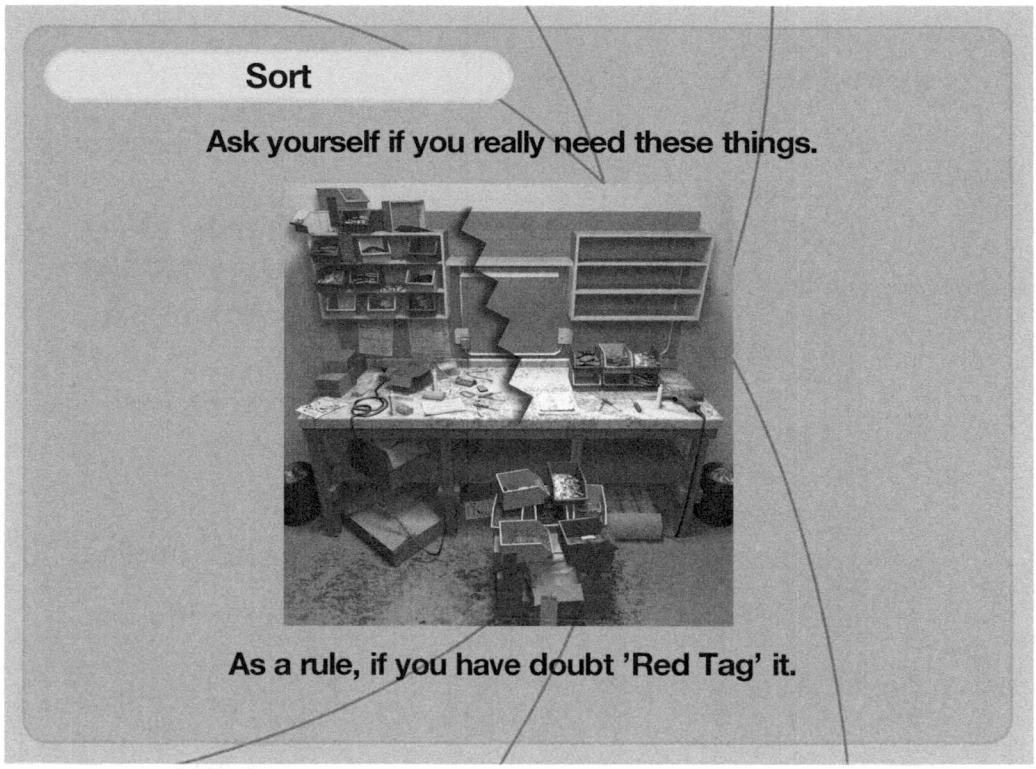

Notes, Slide 18:

Tip:
When sorting, make two categories:
1) what is needed for the job, and
2) everything else.

Sort Action Defined: _____

Additional Example: _____

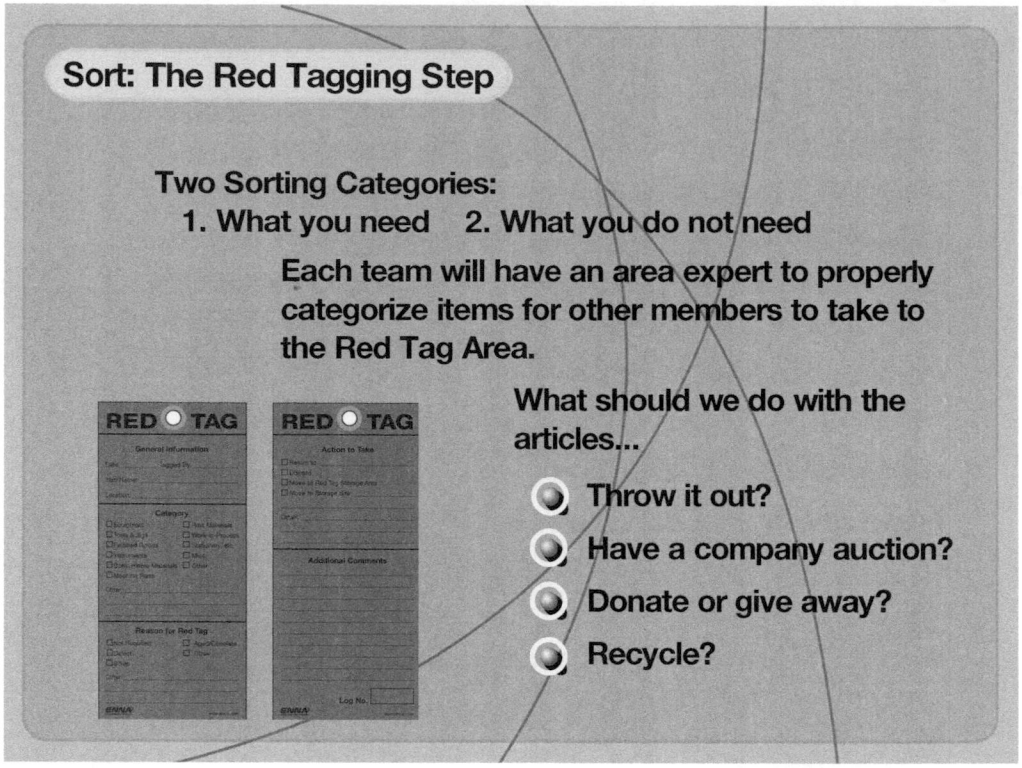

Notes, Slide 19:

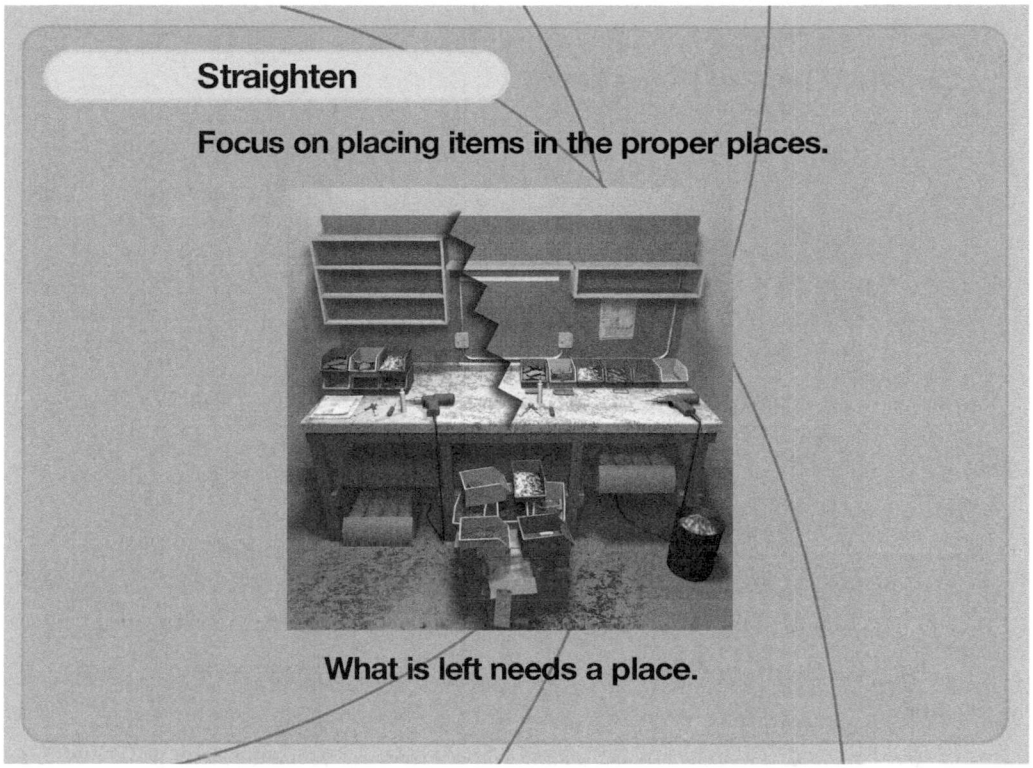

Notes, Slide 20:

_____

_____

_____

_____

Straighten Action Defined: _____

_____

Additional Example: _____

_____

Notes, Slide 21:

Tip:
Look at the above illustration. What work-station solutions can you find that minimize the waste of motion?

Example of Straighten

- Why do auto supply stores position items on shelves?
- Can this apply to what we do?

Notes, Slide 22:

Tip:
Try to reach for anything in your work area. The goal of Straighten is to eliminate reaching.

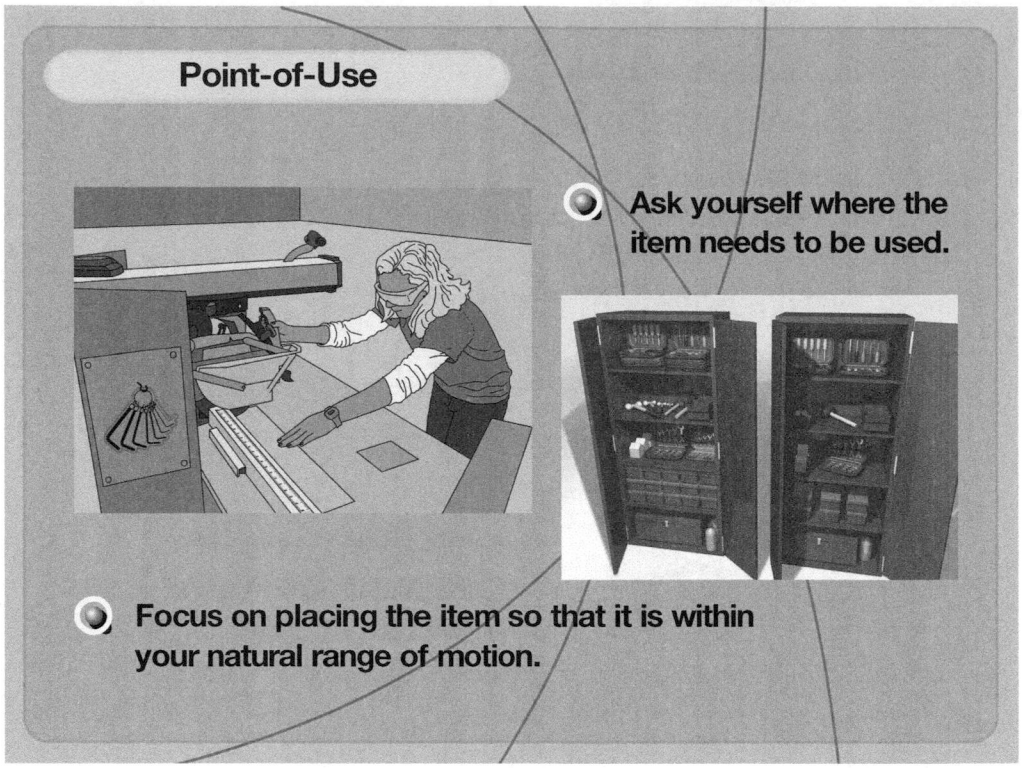

Notes, Slide 23:

Items Have Homes

Are these illustrations good examples of Straighten?

Notes, Slide 24:

Tip:
Use Straighten to get working, rather than just preparing to work.

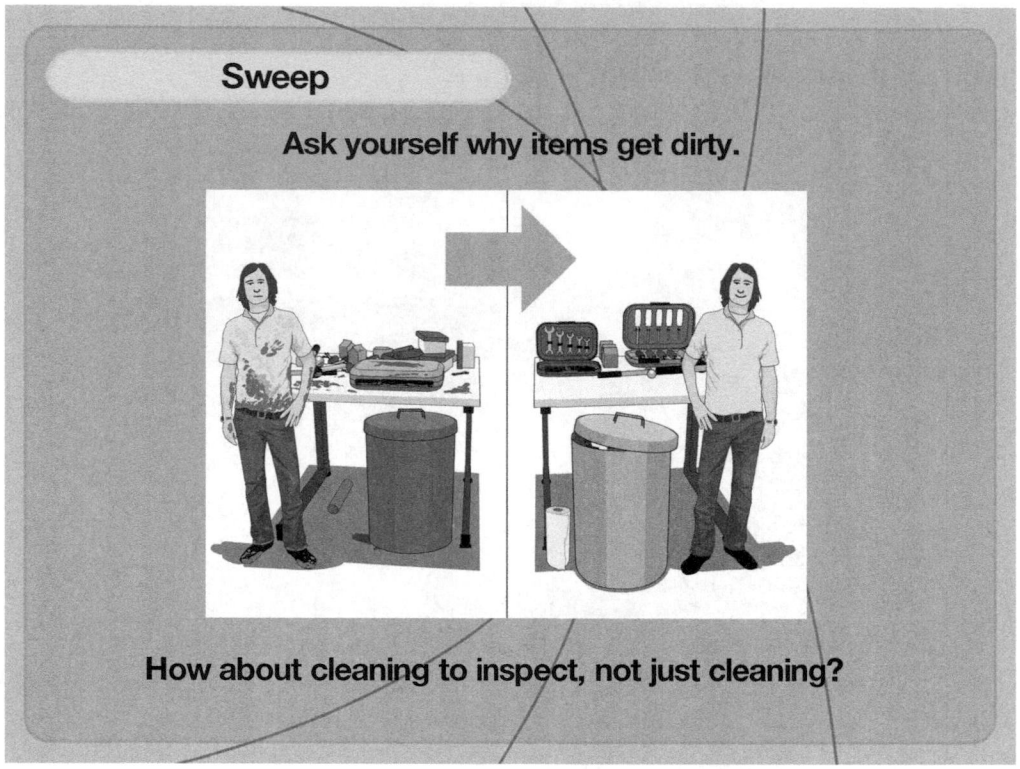

Notes, Slide 25:

_____

_____

_____

_____

_____

_____

Additional Example: _____

_____

Notes, Slide 26:

Tip:
Remember, we are cleaning to...

Sweep Action Defined: _____

Additional Example: _____

Question:

Why are we cleaning during this workshop?

Sweep

Cleaner work environments increase the quality of our work.

Notes, Slide 27:

Tip:
Combining ideas together will find solutions to reducing and even eliminating the need for shining.

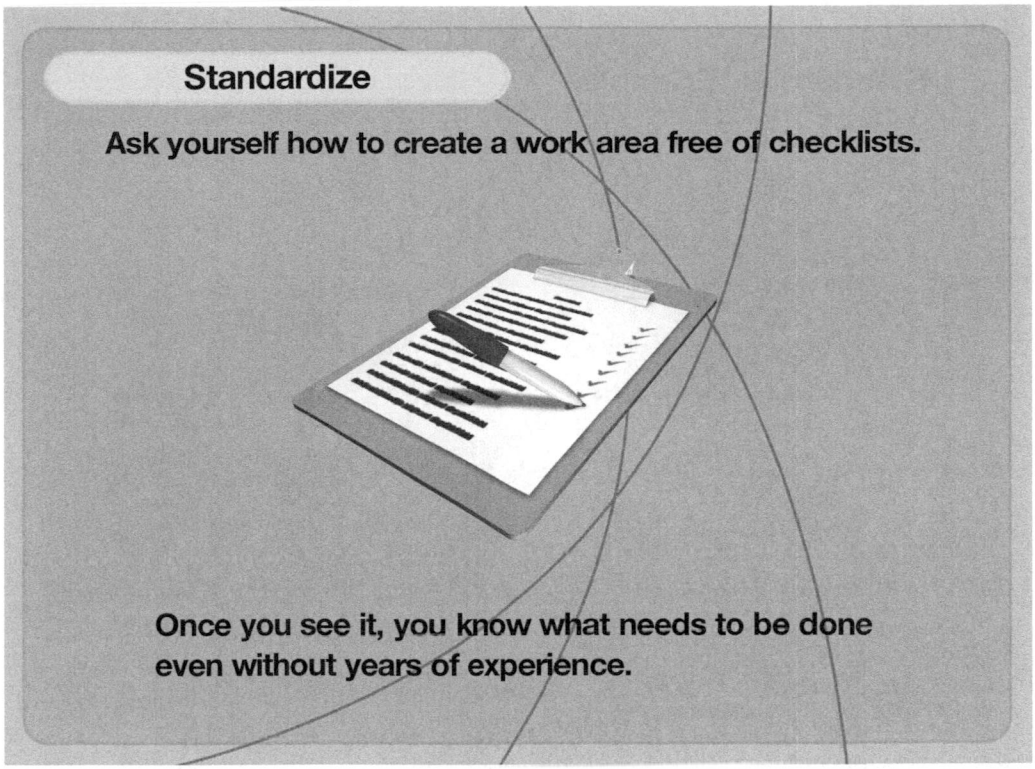

Notes, Slide 28:

Question:

Can you think of an example of good standardization?

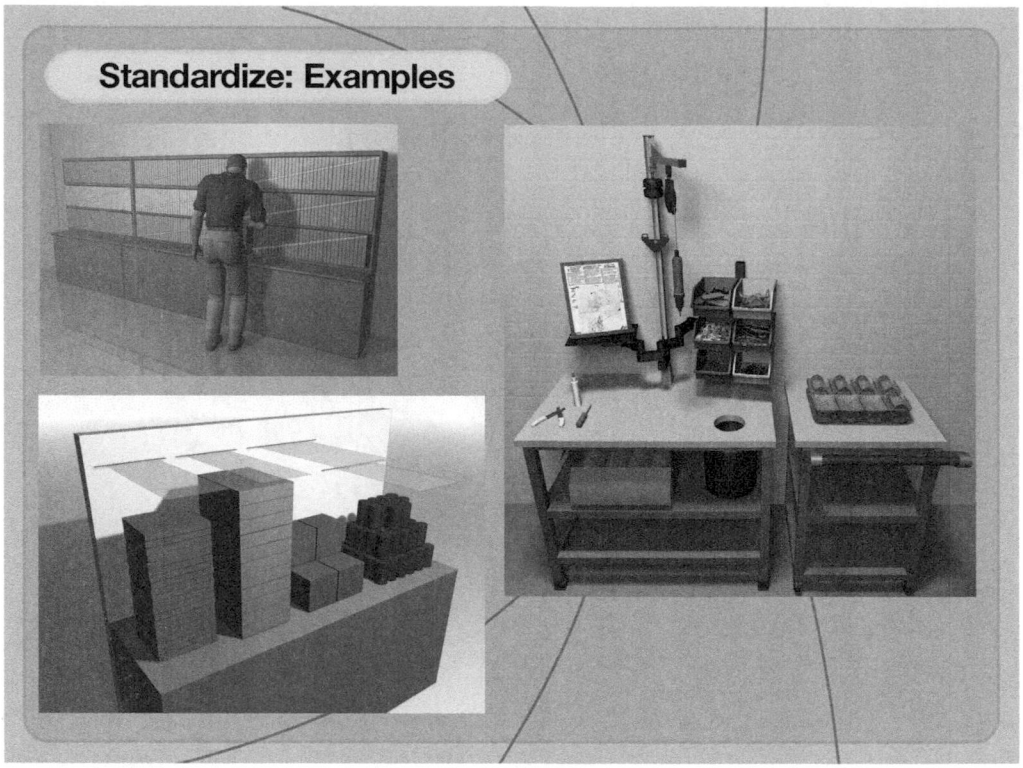

Notes, Slide 29:

_____

_____

_____

_____

Standardize Action Defined: _____

_____

Additional Example: _____

_____

Tip:
When creating a standard, incorporate a symbol, color, and/or physical characteristics.

Sustaining & Cleaning

5S Sustainment Schedule

Start Date: _____ Work Area: _____

Person Responsible	Specific Location	Frequency of Activity	Activities to Perform

Notes, Slide 30:

_____

_____

_____

_____

_____

_____

Question:

Why is it useful to employ the 5S Sustainment Schedule?

_____

_____

_____

Sustain

Keep asking how to simplify the issue to ensure it is sustained.

The idea: if we have less self-discipline it will be easier to sustain.

Notes, Slide 31:

Question:

What is the ultimate goal of 5S?

Sustain

- Management shows commitment to program
- Everyone leads by being an example of 5S
- 5S is a component of every workshop
- Goal is to have customers tour your facility
- Use the Evaluating 5S Forms to assess 5S score

Notes, Slide 32:

_____

_____

_____

_____

Sustain Action Defined: _____

_____

Additional Example: _____

_____

Tip:
Use your past employment experience to help develop sustaining changes. Often past examples help develop solutions. Pull examples from the past and see how the team can use them.

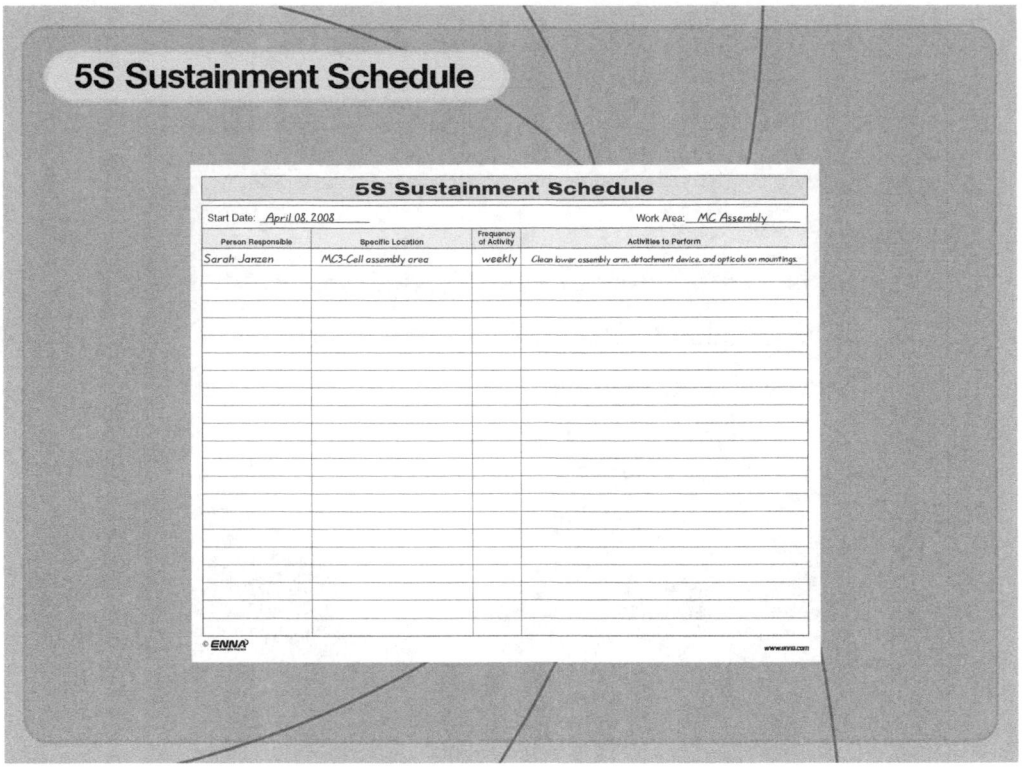

Notes, Slide 33:

Long-Term 5S Success

- Management is expected to be involved in activities
- Involvement of everyone
- 7 Wastes are an integral part of 5S
- Link improvement to a financial benefit

Notes, Slide 34:

Question:

5S needs the commitment of who?

Review & Summary

- What are the 5S words?
- Which S is the most important?
- Can you relate to the need for 5S?
- What are the 7 Wastes?
- What is your responsibility?

Notes, Slide 35:

_____

_____

_____

_____

Final thoughts on this section: _____

_____

_____

Tip:
Write down the answers to these questions to summarize this section.

5S & Teamwork

Participant Workbook

In this Section

Now that we have gained some knowledge we are going to put it into practice.

- Learn the 5S evaluation process
- Learn the 30 Day Action Log
- Learn the 5S Sustainment Schedule
- Discuss the workshop format

Suggestion

Tip

Question

5S Teamwork

Steps:

1: 5S Evaluation

2: Sort- Red Tag Activity

3: Straighten- Point of Use Storage

4: Sweep- Clean Area

5: Standardize- Visual Management

6: Sustain- Refine and Schedule

Notes, Slide 37:

5S Team

1. Evaluating 5S Team (2-3 people)
2. Photography Team (2 people)
   - Take pictures of the current state
   - Highlight key objects and areas
3. 5S Mapping Team (2-3 people)
   - Layout where people, materials, and equipment should be located (bird s eye view)

Notes, Slide 38:

_____

_____

Team Assigned To: _____

_____

Team Members Names: _____

_____

_____

Assigned Work Area:

_____

Additional Information: _____

_____

_____

Tip:
You will change roles as you move from assessment through to making changes, but your team should stay together.

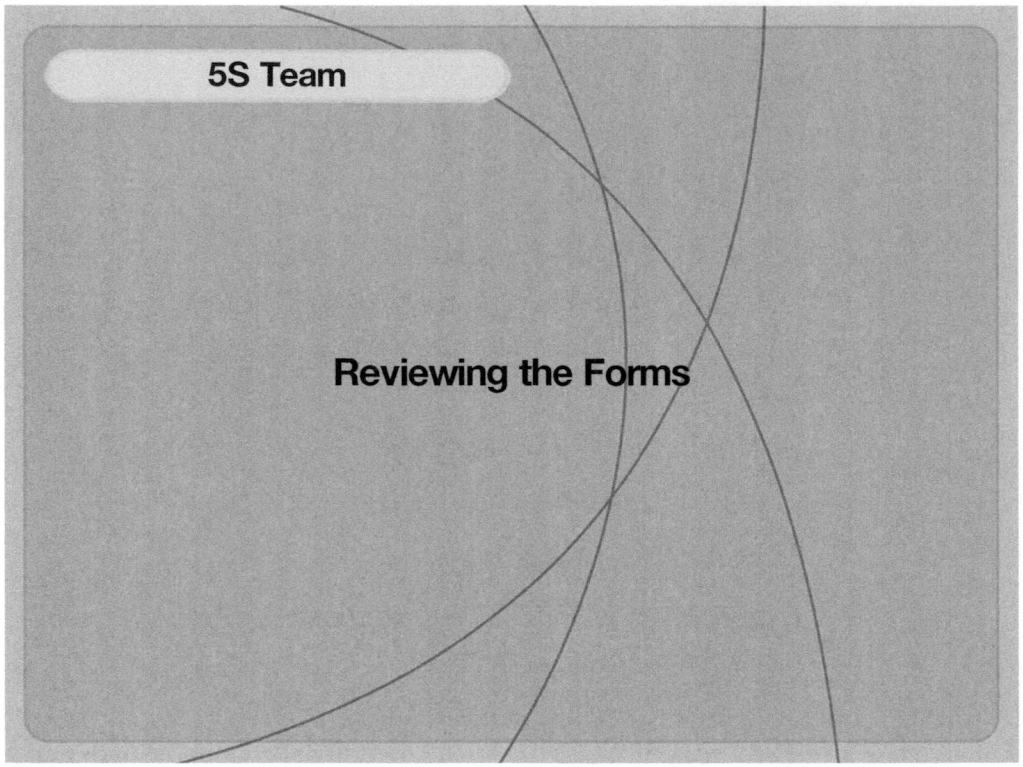

Notes, Slide 39:

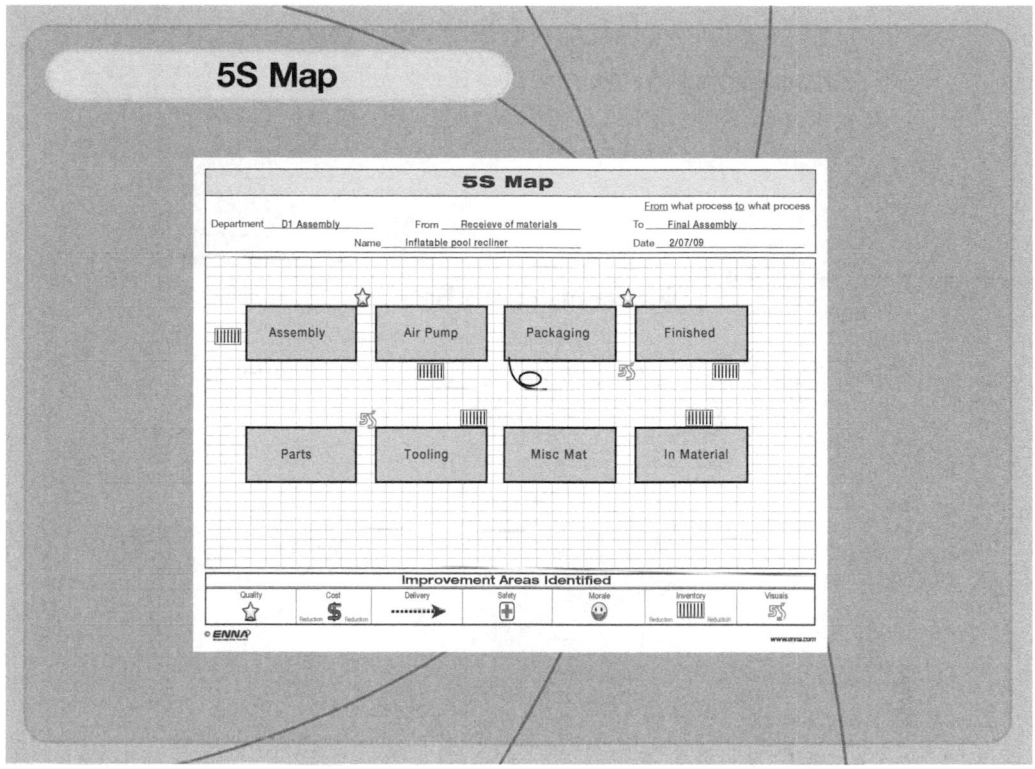

Notes, Slide 40:

5S Evaluation Review

5S Evaluation Review

Date: _____ Evaluation Area: _____

5S Element	Number	Evaluation Criteria	Rank these items from 1 through 5: 5 being well done	Score (1-5)	Ideas / Suggestions / Comments
SORT	I	Are the aisles and walkways open and clear?	All items that are not necessary or unsafe have been removed from the area where people travel and work.		
	II	Is the work zone free of any spills of fluids?	Consider whether there are any chemicals, lubricants, water, oils or other materials that may be hazardous in the area and on the floor.		
	III	Is the work zone free of unnecessary articles and items?	Are items that are not needed been removed from the work zone, i.e. tools, jigs, stationary, extra items.		
	IV	Is the work zone free of excess consumables/materials?	Evaluate against how many items are in the production work zone. Assess if the materials, parts, and supplies are currently needed for operations.		
	V	Is the information board active?	All announcements are displayed currently and in good presentable shape. Arrangement is straight and placed under appropriate headings.		
	VI	Are the areas walls and dividers free of items not used in operations?	Extra items are not on the walls, dividers, or hanging of signs that are not necessary.		
			Category Subtotal		
			Sort Score: Subtotal divided by 6		

Notes, Slide 41:

Tip:

Be critical when evaluating the area; the initial evaluation serves as a baseline for further comparison.

Notes, Slide 42:

Tip:
Lighting is key for photographs. Have the team borrow lights to make the items in the pictures really stand out.

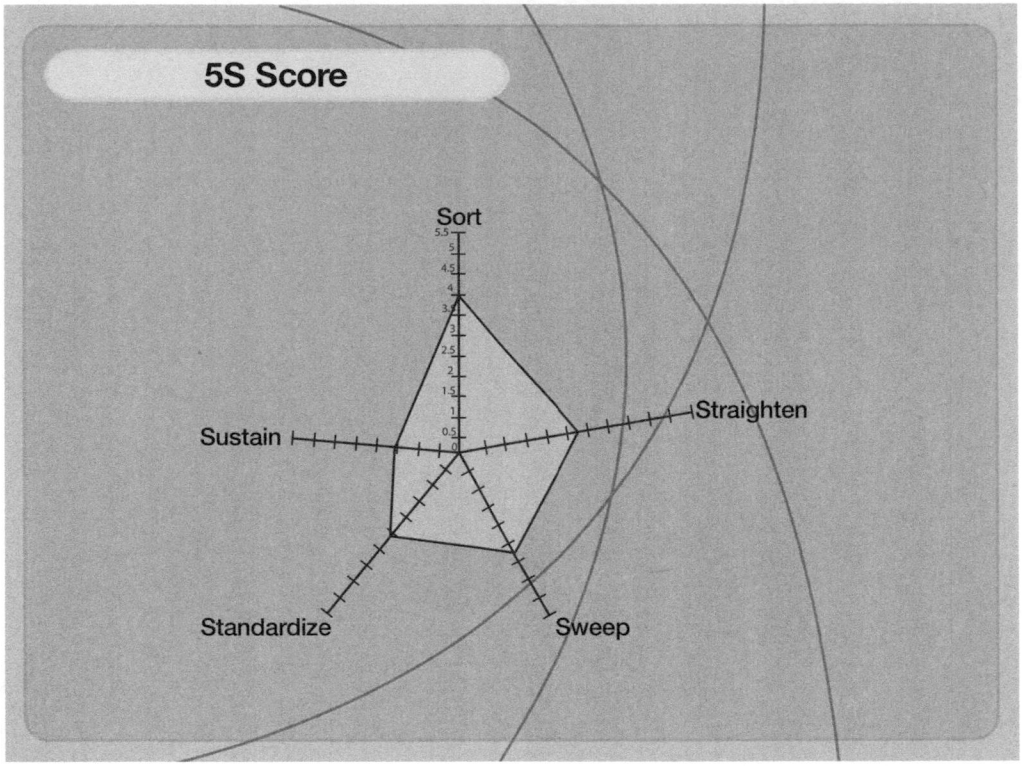

Notes, Slide 43:

Tip:
We should be ready to evaluate our current state.

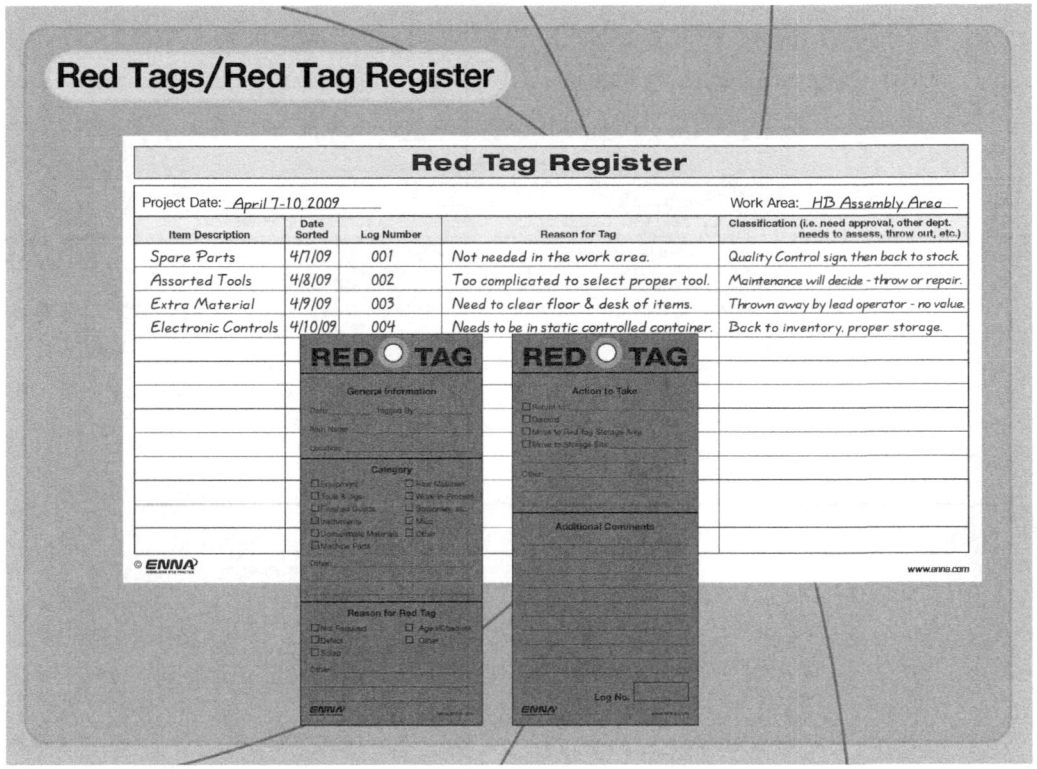

Red Tags/Red Tag Register

Red Tag Register

Project Date: April 7-10, 2009 Work Area: HB Assembly Area

Item Description	Date Sorted	Log Number	Reason for Tag	Classification (i.e. need approval, other dept. needs to assess, throw out, etc.)
Spare Parts	4/7/09	001	Not needed in the work area.	Quality Control sign then back to stock.
Assorted Tools	4/8/09	002	Too complicated to select proper tool.	Maintenance will decide - throw or repair.
Extra Material	4/9/09	003	Need to clear floor & desk of items.	Thrown away by lead operator - no value.
Electronic Controls	4/10/09	004	Needs to be in static controlled container.	Back to inventory, proper storage.

© ENNA www.enna.com

RED TAG

General Information

Category

Reason for Red Tag

RED TAG

Action to Take

Additional Comments

Log No.

Notes, Slide 44 & 45:

Tip:
If you have any doubt, Red Tag it and "throw it out" of the area.

30 Day 5S Action Log

30 Day 5S Action Log

Start Date: 2/10/2010 Work Area: Reassembly

Date Logged	Item Number	5S Problem	Suggestion to Solve Problem	Who is Responsible
2/15/10	1	Empty Parts Caddy's are	Create a Designated Location/Mark/Label/ID	Jared F.
2/17/10	2	Technicians Steal Clean Up Tools	Create End of Day Clean Up Tool	Henry S.
2/20/10	3	Vendors Cannot Find Their	Visually Designate a Return Parts	Troy G.
2/20/10	4	Towels Used for Soaking Up Water	Fix the Leak Near the Receiving Garge Doors	Jan T.
2/22/10	5	Estimates in Teardown are	Implement Visual Incoming and Outgoing	Jared F.

© ENNA www.enna.com

Notes, Slide 46:

Tip:

Only place items on the 30 Day 5S Action Log that the team has agreed is an item for that list. Your team should all agree before adding an item to the 30 Day 5S Action Log. You may have to get support from other departments.

5S Sustainment Schedule

5S Sustainment Schedule

Start Date: April 08, 2008 Work Area: MC Assembly

Person Responsible	Specific Location	Frequency of Activity	Activities to Perform
Sarah Janzen	MC3-Cell assembly area	weekly	Clean lower assembly arm, detachment device, and opticals on mountings.

© ENNA www.enna.com

Notes, Slide 47:

Tip:
Team members are expected to commit to 5S by providing innovative ways to solve problems.

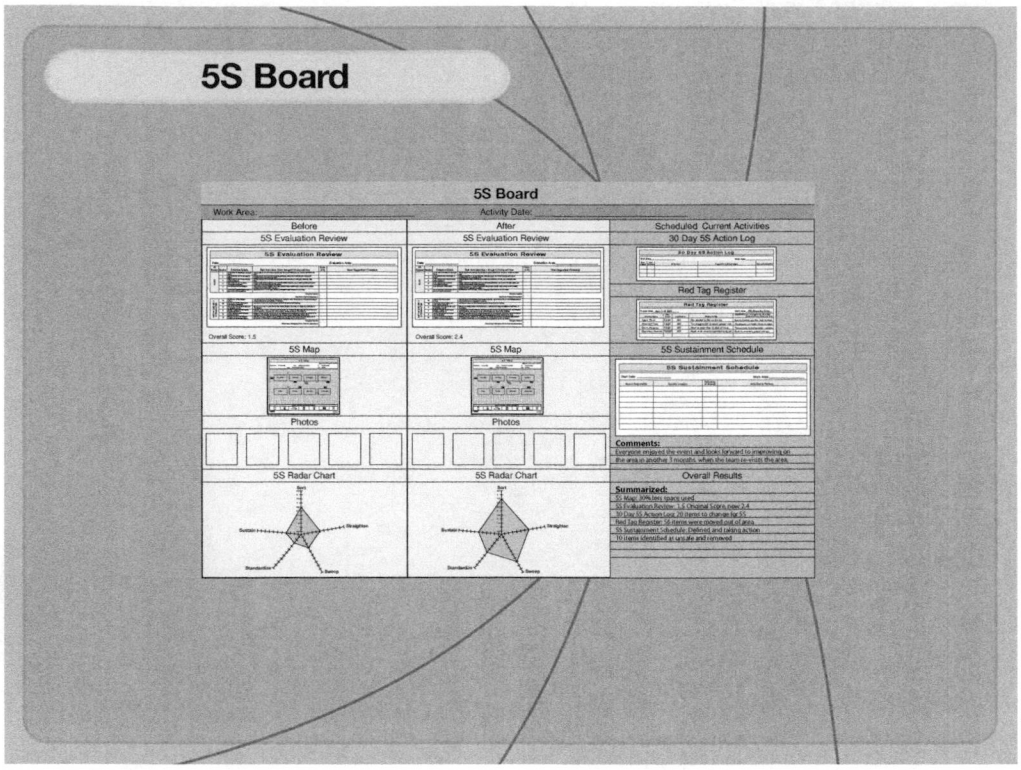

Notes, Slide 48:

5S Assessment

Facilitator: _____ Name: _____

Workshop: _____ Date: _____

Circle or write the answer that best fits the question or completes the statement.

1. 5S originally had S's.
a) 4
b) 1
c) 2

2. What company started what is now known as 5S?
a) Volvo
b) Toyota
c) Ford

3. What is the first S of the 5S's?
a) Straighten
b) Sort
c) Sweep

4. of the 7 Wastes of Operations which one is the worst?
a) Overproduction
b) Inventory
c) Defects

5. If a company implements 5S successfully, the need for self-discipline is .
a) Eliminated
b) Reduced
c) Increased

6. 5S is one of the building blocks of ?
a) Operations
b) Cleanliness
c) Lean

7. Why do we clean during 5S?
a) To inspect
b) Because it is the right thing to do
c) To prevent bad parts

8. What does inventory exist in the company as?
a) Raw, WIP, FG
b) GF, WIP, RAW
c) PIW, WAR, FG

9. The S in Straighten allows for a person to have minimal .
a) Work
b) Waiting
c) Motion

10. What is the 5S Sustainment Schedule used for?
a) Recording workshop activity
b) Recording the cleaning that is needed
c) Scheduling the next workshop

11. For 5S to be successful we need the involvement of .
a) Top management
b) Entire department
c) Everyone

12. The 5S Map provides a simple point of view of the work area.
a) Bird's eye
b) Planning
c) Outline

13. Processing is the hardest waste to find because .
a) There are so many processes
b) It may initially seem to be a value-added step
c) It is totally necessary

14. The 30-Day Action Log allows the company to .
a) Document a list of unsolvable problems
b) List workshop problems to be solved on one document
c) Demonstrate its commitment to 5S

1:c, 2:b, 3:b, 4:a, 5:b, 6:c, 7:a, 8:a, 9:c, 10:b, 11:c, 12:a, 13:b, 14:b

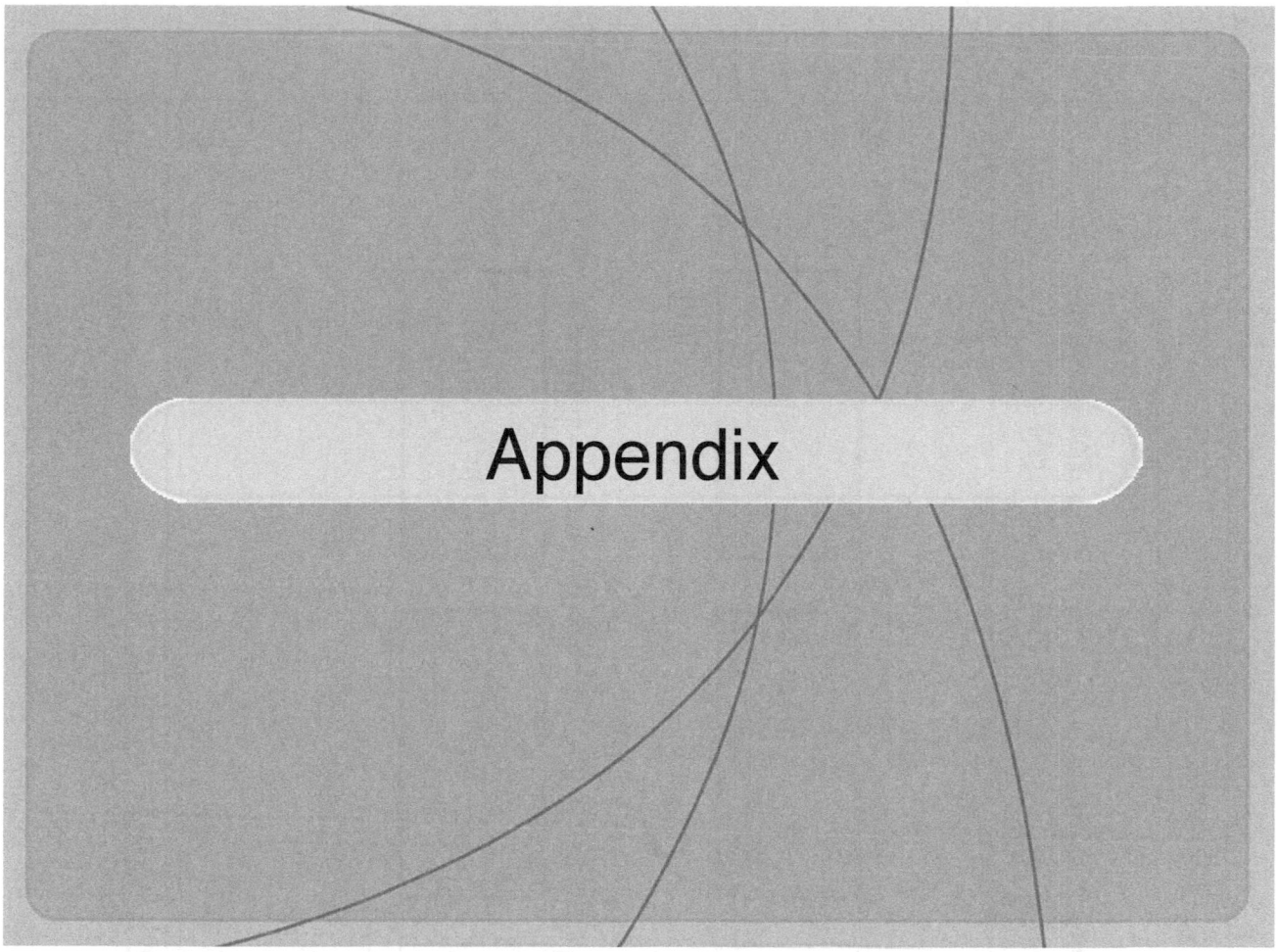

Participant Workbook

In this Section

You will find copies of the forms used in the workshop filled out for your reference.

5S Map

From what process to what process

Department D1 Assembly From Receieve of materials To Final Assembly

Name Inflatable pool recliner Date 2/07/09

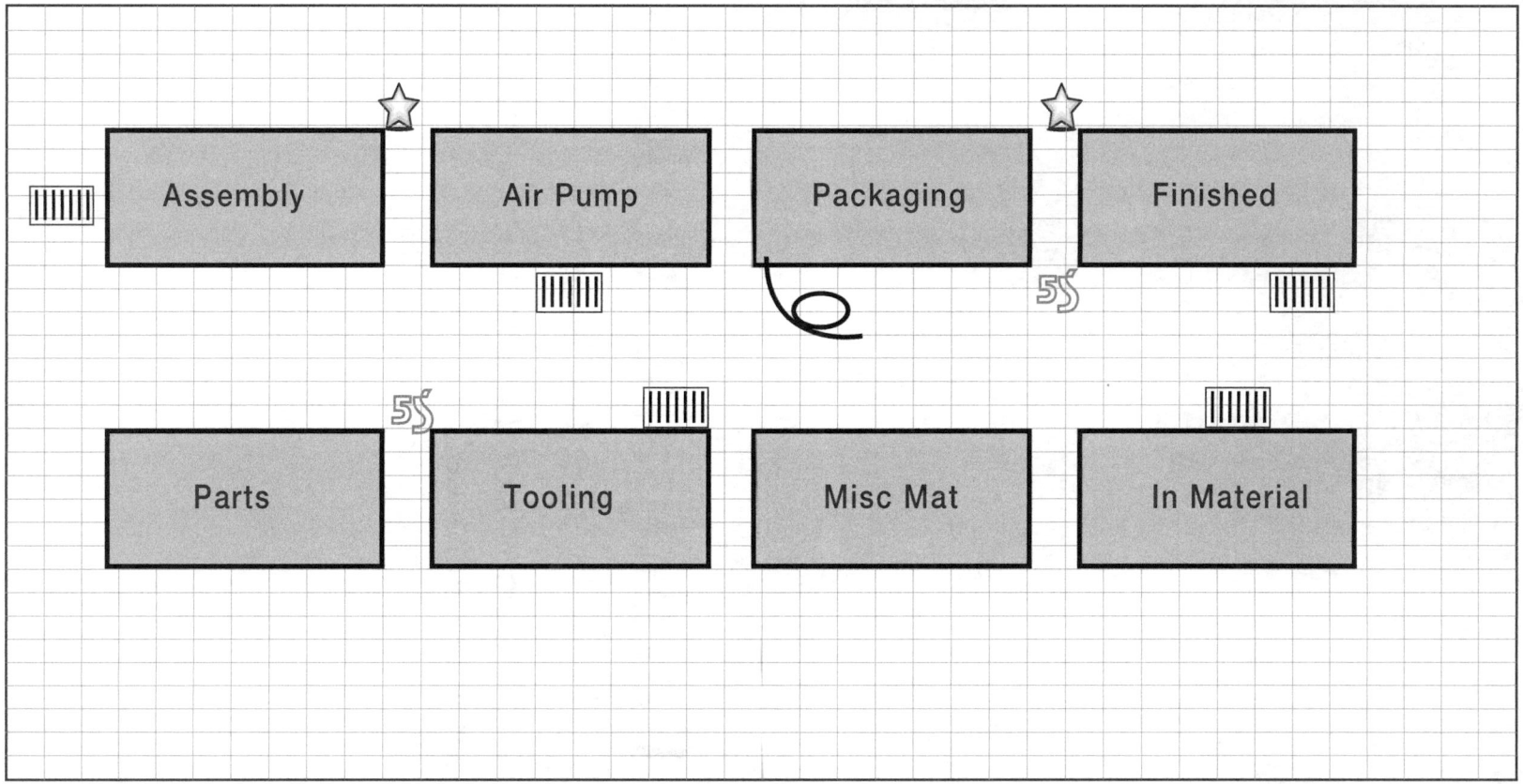

Improvement Areas Identified

Quality	Cost	Delivery	Safety	Morale	Inventory	Visuals
	Reduction Reduction				Reduction Reduction	

© ENNA KNOWLEDGE INTO PRACTICE

5S Evaluation Review

Date: _____ Evaluation Area: _____

5S Element	Number	Evaluation Criteria	Rank these items from 1 through 5: 5 being well done	Score (1-5)	Ideas / Suggestions / Comments
SORT	I	Are the aisles and walkways open and clear?	All items that are not necessary or unsafe have been removed from the area where people travel and work.		
	II	Is the work zone free of any spills of fluids?	Consider whether there are any chemicals, lubricants, water, oils or other materials that may be hazardous in the area and on the floor.		
	III	Is the work zone free of unnecessary articles and items?	Are items that are not needed been removed from the work zone, i.e. tools, jigs, stationary, extra items.		
	IV	Is the work zone free of excess consumables/materials?	Evaluate against how many items are in the production work zone. Assess if the materials, parts, and supplies are currently needed for operations.		
	V	Is the information board active?	All announcements are displayed currently, and in good presentable shape. Arrangement is straight and placed under appropriate headings.		
	VI	Are the areas walls and dividers free of items not used in operations?	Extra items are not on the walls, dividers, or hanging of signs that are not necessary.		
			Category Subtotal		
			Sort Score: Subtotal divided by 6		

Red Tag Register

Project Date: April 7-10, 2009 Work Area: HB Assembly Area

Item Description	Date Sorted	Log Number	Reason for Tag	Classification (i.e. need approval, other dept. needs to assess, throw out, etc.)
Spare Parts	4/7/09	001	Not needed in the work area.	Quality Control sign, then back to stock.
Assorted Tools	4/8/09	002	Too complicated to select proper tool.	Maintenance will decide - throw or repair.
Extra Material	4/9/09	003	Need to clear floor & desk of items.	Thrown away by lead operator - no value.
Electronic Controls	4/10/09	004	Needs to be in static controlled container.	Back to inventory, proper storage.

30 Day 5S Action Log

Start Date: 2/10/2010 Work Area: Reassembly

Date Logged	Item Number	5S Problem	Suggestion to Solve Problem	Who is Responsible
2/15/10	1	Empty Parts Caddy's are	Create a Designated Location/Mark/Label/ID	Jared F.
2/17/10	2	Technicians Steal Clean Up Tools	Create End of Day Clean Up Tool	Henry S.
2/20/10	3	Vendors Cannot Find Their	Visually Designate a Return Parts	Troy G.
2/20/10	4	Towels Used for Soaking Up Water	Fix the Leak Near the Receiving Garge Doors	Jan T.
2/22/10	5	Estimates in Teardown are	Implement Visual Incoming and Outgoing	Jared F.

© ENNA KNOWLEDGE INTO PRACTICE

5S Sustainment Schedule

Start Date: April 08, 2008

Work Area: MC Assembly

Person Responsible	Specific Location	Frequency of Activity	Activities to Perform
Sarah Janzen	MC3-Cell assembly area	weekly	Clean lower assembly arm, detachment device, and opticals on mountings.

© ENNA
KNOWLEDGE INTO PRACTICE

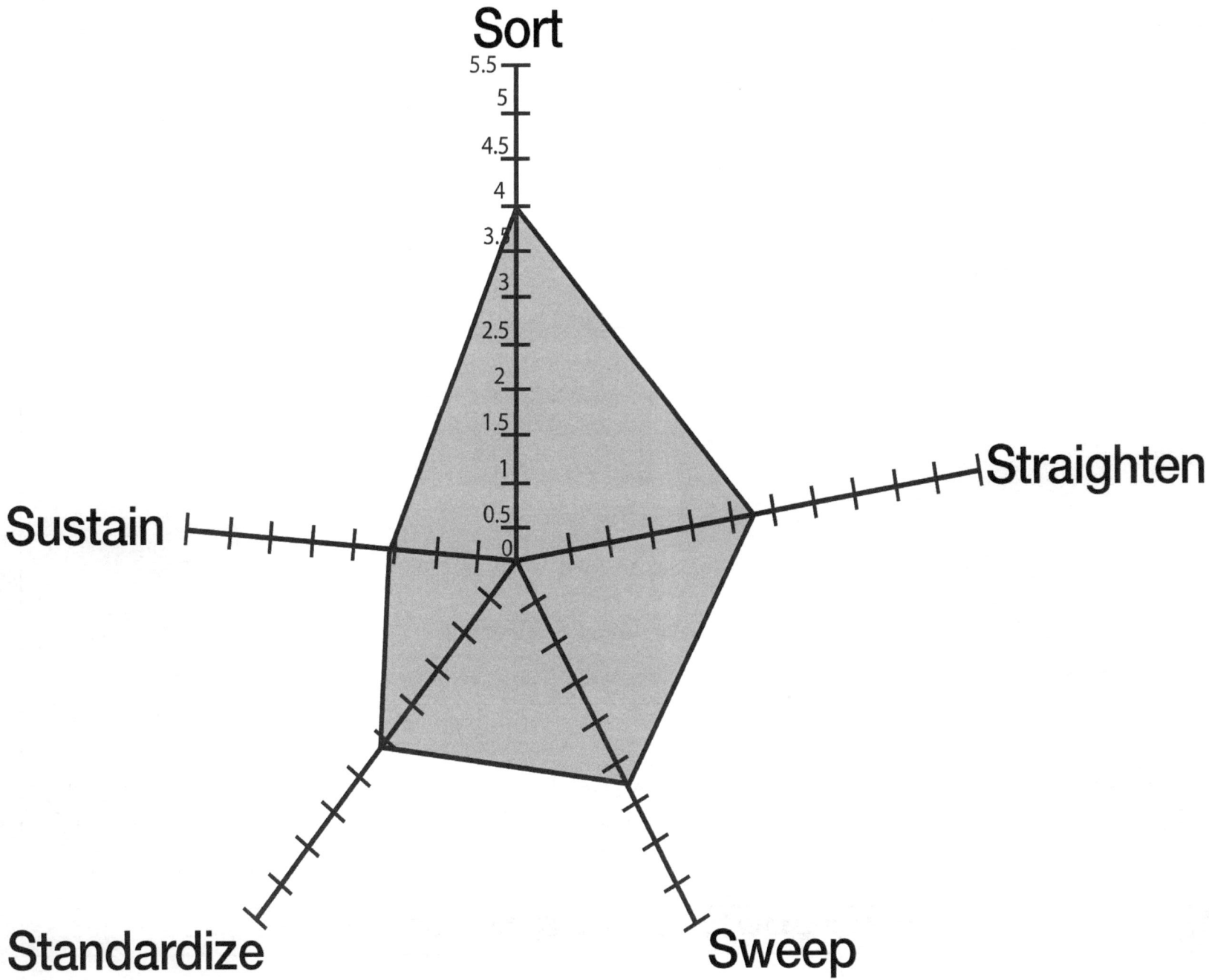
Sort
5.5
5
4.5
4
3.5
3
2.5
2
1.5
1
0.5
0
Straighten
Sweep
Standardize
Sustain

9781138069299

9781138069299